THE DIARY OF A SILENCE

By the same author:

Poetry

Stalingrad: The Street Dictionary
(Raven Arts Press, 1980)

Atlantic Blues
(Raven Arts Press, 1982)

Criticism

— Patrick Kavanagh & the discourse of contemporary
Irish Poetry
(Raven Arts Press, 1985)

Michael O'Loughlin

THE DIARY OF A SILENCE

RAVEN ARTS PRESS

This book is published by

THE RAVEN ARTS PRESS
P.O. Box 1430
Finglas
Dublin 11
Ireland

Raven Arts Press receives financial assistance from the Arts Council/
An Chomhairle Ealaíon, Dublin, Ireland.

Acknowledgements are made to the editors of the following, where
some of these poems first appeared: *Aquarius* , *The Beau, The Irish
Times, North, 2plus2* (Lausanne) and *An tÉireannach* (Paris).

A number of these poems were originally published, along with a
selection of poems by Dermot Bolger, in *A New Primer for Irish
Schools,* published in a limited edition in 1985 to mark the 50th
Raven title.

The writer acknowledges the assistance of Bursaries from the Arts
Council/An Chomhairle Ealaíon, in 1982 and 1984, which helped
greatly towards the completion of this volume.

ISBN 1 85186 000 2

Cover photograph, "Night Fire" by Bob Glaubit. Cover design by Susanne
Linde. Typesetting by Máire Davitt, Vermilion. Design by Dermot Bolger.

CONTENTS

For Judith

I

AN IRISH REQUIEM
(i.m. Mary Lynch (1897-1983)

Born in another country, under a different flag
She did not die before her time
Her god never ceased to speak to her.
And so she did not die. The only death that is real
Is when words change their meaning
And that is a death she never knew
Born in another country, under a different flag
When the soldiers and armoured cars
Spilled out of the ballads and onto the screen
Filling the tiny streets, she cried
And wiped her eyes on her apron, mumbling something
About the Troubles. That was a word
I had learned in my history book.
What did I care for the wails of the balding Orpheus
As he watched Eurydice burn in hell?
I was eleven years old,
And my Taoiseach wrote to me,
Born in another country, under a different flag.
She did not die before her time
But went without fuss, into the grave
She had bought and tended herself, with
The priest to say rites at her entry
And the whole family gathered,
Black suits and whiskey, a cortege
Of Ford Avengers inching up the cemetery hill.
Death came as an expected visitor,
A policeman, or rate collector, or the tinker
Who called every spring for fresh eggs,
Announced by the season, or knocks on walls,
Bats flying in and out of rooms, to signify
She did not die before her time
Her god never ceased to speak to her.
Till the last, he murmured in her kitchen
As she knelt at the chair beside the range

Or moved to the damp, unused, parlour
For the priest's annual visit.
Poete de sept ans, I sat on the polished wood,
Bored by the priest's vernacular harangue
As she knelt beside me on the stone church floor,
And overheard her passionate whisper,
Oblivious, telling her beads, and I knew
That I would remember this, that
Her god never ceased to speak to her.
And so she did not die. The only death that is real
Is when words change their meaning
And that is a death she never knew.
As governments rose and fell, she never doubted
The name of the land she stood on. Nothing
But work and weather darkened the spring days
When she herded her fattened cattle
Onto the waiting cars. It is not she who haunts
But I, milking her life for historical ironies,
Knowing that more than time divides us.
But still her life burns on, like the light
From a distant, extinguished star, and
O let me die before that light goes out
Born in another country, under a different flag!

II

THE SHARDS
a poem sequence

"In the North we are not only on the cold edge of civilisation, but also on that of being, truth and life itself. Naked imaginative field . . . "

— Asger Jorn

I. THE BUNKERS

Along the great coast south of Bordeaux
The bunkers still stare out to sea
High-water marks of the black wave
That swept up out of the sump of Europe.
Untouched, they stand, undying monuments,
Easter Island heads in cold concrete.
On the side of one I found
Some Gothic lettering, black paint
That hadn't faded in the years of sun and wind.
But the blonde naked daughters
Sleep rough in them during the summer nights
And in the morning run laughing
Into the ocean their fathers had scanned.

II. THE BIRDS

Somewhere north of Lille
I stared at the sea of white crosses,
Like sea birds resting on the earth.
So much suddenly real!

III. FRANK RYAN DEAD IN DRESDEN!

The idea armed, like Ernie O'Malley
Another emerald-green incorruptible
Of course there was no place for the likes of you!
When you came bounding out of the prison camps
To join the shuffling battalions
Into the civil service offices
They gave you a job writing tourist brouchures.
"Killarney is famous the wide world over
for the magnificent splendour
of its mountains and lakes . . . "
And after, you marched off into the night
To practise the illegal alchemy
Of slogans and heavy printer's ink.
Now it speeds up. A handsome head, in uniform.
Then defeat. The tale grows complex.
Europe dividing under your feet.
Conspiracies, betrayals, and all the rest.
In that last passport photo taken in Berlin
You look like Rembrandt in his last self-portrait.
There is much there I don't know, nor want to.
You followed your river into the sea,
And drowned, while your funeral pyre
Lit up the skies for a hundred miles around.

IV. FROM A DIARY

I seem to have travelled this landscape for years.
Brown hulks of deserted factories, the dark wounds
Of their shattered windows, fragments of glass
Defying the wind. The yellow blocks of flats
And behind them, the endless ordered fields
Flecked with rusted iron.
The train slowed down near a flat broad river
And I saw fields full of green machines
Stretching out into the distance,
Tensing on black rubber. A lone sentry
Stood out against the skyline, looking in no
Particular direction. Behind him a filthy grey sky
Floundered into the night.

V. HEINRICH BÖLL IN IRELAND

We slept through it. A stray bomber,
A black sheep strayed from the pack
Came crackling in out of the watching darkness.
Later, some stumbled across our shores
In search of a green poultice
For wounds we couldn't have understood.
There, at last, a small destiny, ours.
This also; the skyways criss-crossed
By peaceful jets, their passengers reading
In magazines about the
Most profitable
Industrial
Location
In Europe.

VI. CONCERT-GOING IN VIENNA

Our houses are open tombs that will survive us.
And so are our lives. No one survives a war like that.
That is obvious; also ridiculous.
Our eyes blink in the sullen gleam of the knife
But do not see the submerged balancing weight
Beneath the cutting edge. Tonight, I feel it
The solid drag, the tug and undertow
Of centuries of prosperity, watching
These faces and manners planed by music,
I had not thought death had missed so many.
This woman here in front of me, for instance
In pearls and grey hair in a stately bun
Nodding her head in time to Bruckner's Fourth.
She is not dead, nor am I. The sublime
And gracious she samples as familiar delicacies
And it is churlish of me to criticise this.
But still, I know, from the ranks of satisfied diners
A hungry ghost slips off into the forest
Trying on coats of clay for size.

VII. THE BOYS OF '69

"I don't know why we didn't go —
we talked about nothing else."
But they didn't go, didn't die
On the barricades of '69,
They survived to cushy jobs
In Luxembourg and Brussels.
Cushy but hopeless!
"Sure we hadn't a chance boy!
What do you think?
The French and the Dutch
were already dug in."
He peels the silver wrapping
Off another bottle of beer.
I watch the alien sun sink red
Behind the blocks of flats.
"Poor Sean! They found his body
out there on the beach. Nothing
ever proved, of course. Never
saw him depressed. A boy
to drink though! He was barred
from the British Embassy
after that night,
I remember it well . . . "
I suddenly see him, poor Sean,
With his Aran sweater
And second-class degree in history
A pale-faced corpse
Drifting like a dead fish
Through a sea of foreign newsprint
Red-bearded idol of a scattered army
Of terylene shirts and expense accounts
In half the capital cities of Europe . . .

VIII. THE SHARDS

For months, coming home late at night
We would stop at a traffic light
In the middle of nowhere
And sit there, the engine restless
For the empty motorway
While I looked out at the half-built flyover
That stood in the moonlight
Like a ruined Greek temple
And I suddenly felt surrounded
By the shattered and potent monuments
Of a civilisation we have not yet discovered
The ghost of something stalking us
The future imagined past perhaps
Or else the millions of dead
Rising and falling
Into the mud and carved stone
The ghost of the beast
Whose carapace we inhabit
Not knowing if we stand
At centre or circumference
Sensing that shards are our only wholeness
Carefully carving their shattered edges.

III

" . . . the whole world is suburb
Where are the real towns?"

— Marina Tsetaeva.

IN THE SUBURBS

I.   A Letter To Marina Tsetaeva

In white rooms looking out on the city
I woke up alone with you, Marina Tsetaeva.
Her body is a sheet of cold white flame
Where I am burned to translucence;
In her hair I smelt Prague and damnation
And music tearing through flesh
Like the pull of a planet.
Her mocking schoolgirl's laugh
Her arched dancer's calf
Her feet in white boots like elegant hooves!

Who else
Could I pray
To watch over her
In the darkness where she moves.

2. The Music Lesson

In white rooms looking out on the city
Filled with light like flat champagne
We woke to that aboriginal heat
And walked out into the warm rain.

It sprinkled its dusty benediction
On the Sunday morning pavements
Streaked the windows of our train
Through the passionate clay of the mountains.

When we reached the town I left you behind
Walked out into the almond trees
And sat in the dust in the dead afternoon
Surrounded by my own emptiness

Watching the distant mountain range
Whose name I couldn't remember
Feeling everything drop away
Into the static sweating air.

With the year dying all around me, I walked
Back to the house where I'd left you singing
Like a man approaching his execution
For a cause he no longer believed in.

I turned away into the future
And watched you go
Like a man stepping through
A plate-glass window.

3. In the Suburbs

Closing my eyes I sink down into a darkness
Where your absence is the only presence.
Open again to a shout of light
Two lip-sticked girls, a glass of beer
Push you back into fragile limits.
I leave the bar and move out
Into the raw streets of this half-built suburb
Stepping over virgin pavements
And violated earth
Through a mesh of lives just beginning
And I'm the only prisoner
Of this heavy spring evening, this dull suburb
Unable to mortgage my life to the future.

4. The Knot

When a note is played
The pause that follows
Is no longer silence.

FROM A CAFÉ

"Fósforo y fósforo en la oscuridad,
lagrima y lagrima en la polvareda."
— César Vallejo

Last night I dreamt you were in my room.
In my sleep I felt your presence
Like fine rain on my nerve ends
But when I struggled awake you were gone.

You've blown through me like nuclear fallout
And left me reeling, sick in my bones
Nursing my sickness in suburban cafés
Where the coffee bubbles with faith in mankind.

Match after match in the dark
Tear after tear in the dust
The waitress brings me cup after cup
While I hide my face in a foreign tongue.

ON BOARD

I see you asleep in our old room
The soft shine of your hands
And eyelids, like a fish's belly
In a dark ocean.

Outside, lit up
And throbbing with emptiness
The city pads through the night
Like a great space station.

The waves
Of your sleeping body
Rise and fall
On my mind's ragged edge.

Hours ago,
I peeled away from your side
Hurtled off
Into outer darkness

But left my poetry
To watch over your bed
A black angel
Caught in the mesh of your hair.

IN A BATHROOM

Venus emerging from a porcelain shell
You step out of the bath, and stand there, dripping
With a towel wrapped tight about your head
Your face deathly white in a beauty mask.

A carnal nun, angst in high heels.
You always look the way I feel
With your mouth twisted by music
Your nails stained with the blood of lies!

I sit here watching you move about
Thinking of how I love you
But can think of nothing but Lorca
And the smell of the sun on my leather jacket.

THE CHORD

We stand in an ocean
Of melted light. It is dusk.
The smell of eucalyptus
On the chilled city air
The glow of streetlights
Behind the dark leaves.
You bow your head before me
Under a pain I can't understand.
That I have caused it
I sense dimly, like an animal
Or a man looking at a painting
By some old master,
Full of forgotten allegory.
I am silent,
Appalled at my own existence
Unable to move an inch
Away from you,
Or nearer.

POSTHUMOUS

Something is pushing against my blood.
From the bus I watch the children
Set fire to sheets of paper
And scatter them, screaming, into the wind.
They burn down to nothing,
A black smudge on the concrete
Bleeding its greyness into the sky.
I think of Siberia, how clean it is.
I move around the city, denounced
To the secret police of popular songs.
A name flares in the darkness.
Moon-sister, twin.
Who are you? I don't know.
My mouth tastes of splintered bone.
I thought I'd left this place a long time ago.

IV

"La source est roc et la langue est tranchée"
— Rene Char

THE DIARY OF A SILENCE

In Parnell Square it's always raining
On the junk heap of history where I was born
One wet night, in the Rotunda Hospital
While the crowds surged down O'Connell Street
And the shades did cluster round
My state-assisted birth, in this elephant's
Graveyard under grey skies!

The damp, disintegrating houses
Shuffle shoulder to shoulder through time
Stuffed with religious statues and creaking
Rooms, empty, forgotten, memorial halls
Marked by cracked plaques and faded signs
Of chipped gilt over fanlights
Everything living its posthumous existence
Hungering in me for an image
That is not mere archaeology
The casual coupling of history and self.

I probed the city's cracked grey ribs,
Noted the casual irony
Of the tottering Georgian tenements!
But one day they were gone
Thesis devoured by antithesis
Oratory swallowed by irony
Cancelling each other out
Leaving not even an aftertaste
Just silence tensing towards the word
That will define it,
In a language that doesn't yet exist.

Where the buildings once had stood
The sky rushed into their virgin spaces
The mad light of Dublin battering my face
The great expressionist winter sky

Where light and dark wrestle like primitive gods
Like complex chemical formulae
Something struggling to become itself.

It has always been like this. What can be said
Is not worth saying, will not still the itch
That has always possessed me, gripped
And held fast from the start
And would not release, or burst into flower
Except suddenly, laboriously,
Like turning the corner into Parnell Square
To see the yellow buses throbbing in the rain
Pristine, orphic; obmutescent.

TWO POEMS FOR PADDY GRAHAM

1.   Summer in Monaghan

my mouth is daubed with black and green!
gulping mouthfuls of dark air
black flags hang from the telegraph poles
this land is a hunger
I cannot breathe
love lies like a plague on the land
love? the greyness of summer?
(who are those faces, bright
and I think, familiar,
names, old loves, stirring
like nails in their rusty sockets)

a black sea rocks us to sleep

in the morning the darkness lightens
between the murderous drumlins
the roads are smeared
with small furred corpses
sometimes a sweet rain rinses the air
water colours a faint illusion
(in the dead hiss of a summer's evening
a lake has drifted from Persia)

2. Heimat

All over Ireland the black light falls.
On the rotting stone houses of
Provincial towns,
And on the pristine office blocks;
On the nervous green fields
And cold suburban roads.
This was home, as a child I knew it.
The black clouds soaked in radiance
Exploding softly on the Wicklow Mountains
Marching west in a dinosaur train
Across the wet slate roofs, bobbing
Heavily forward with brute momentum
And grace, leaving their footprints
In my mind, deserts hungry
For remembered weather,
Like your canvas hungry for paint
Each painting a difficult homecoming
A muddy thaw, savage archaeology, the slow
Decolonisation of childhood,
Letting us see
What is in the black light visible.

THE SMILE

Late summer. A Dublin Sunday,
hushed and heavy
my soles scrape the pavement

There was a smell
of burning rubber
from the park behind the flats

A policeman on a motorbike
zig-zagged
the afternoon streets

a remote-control toy
smudging the air
with demon voices

A young man with a mexican moustache
stood casual guard
as two children played in the gutter

I approached from a long way off
to ask him the way;
he answered slowly

as I watched the phoenix
sketched
on the chest of his t-shirt

"Never heard of it. But
I'll tell you this much.
It's nowhere near this kip."

And we smiled
like the future regarding the past
or vice versa

ETYMOLOGIES

"I'll reef him —
I'll take his bleedin' life . . . "
hurrying through
the threatening streets
of childhood
bound for home
things half-overheard
half-remembered
come back into my mind
now late at night
as I trace
those streets again
along the map of words
bludgeoning
my way home
with dubious etymologies
reefed by that place
where the dictionaries
hit the streets

SHIBBOLETH

Third world suburb,
Baking in october heat.
Stepping up out of the metro
The air swabs my back.
The streets are poor, unpaved
the brandy cheap in the bars.
I'm the only thing that moves
in the dust and heat of the afternoon
always reluctant to leave
when the day's work was done
a sweating amnesiac revenant
dawdling along the streets
a child dossing home from school
clutching a book
he can't yet read.

Each day I passed
the old-fashioned steelworks
squinted to read the slogans
on the walls of the yellow
jerry-built flats;
stopped at a bar
to wolf down cokes
and listen to the furnace roar
of the city-bound traffic
out on the avenida: Sagrera!

I have learned this suburb by heart
I have learned a word
that I couldn't translate
even to myself.

THREE FRAGMENTS ON THE THEME
OF MOVING AROUND IN CITIES

I. Epitaph for Matt Talbot

"Skua!" "Skua!", the gulls shriek
Skitting above the stinking Liffey
Where your name flaps
Like a plastic sack
Along the deserted quays
In the minds of old women
Carrying their shopping
From chapel to chapel.

II. Little Suburban Ode

In our cold, gloomy Napoli
Pasolini's Nordic children
Cruise the icy pot-holed streets
In stolen diplomatic limos

Rocketing round the broken corners
Like steel balls in a pinball game
Before they fly right off the board
— Or slot home safely in the suburbs.

III. Berlin

Under a bruised sky the empires meet
And freeze. I don't like that I like it here,
The cold stench of flesh become stone
The palled appalling innocence of the heart
A giddy dog loping through ruins
A god on the morning of creation
His mouth full of juicy bones.

ONE VERSION OF A MYTH

I scribbled poems
in the back of
my chemistry notebook
about the survival
of primitive man
into the techno-
logical era.
But they didn't
answer my question.
At evening I always
found myself here
in one place or another
watching the dusk descend
on the shuttered suburbs
splash the skyline
with chemical red
and then
the light was gone —
suddenly swallowed
by billowing clouds
of octopus black —
tomorrow it would return
in lines
of field-grey infantry
straggling in
across the coast road
and the frozen sand
choked on the corpses
of birds
and old rubber tyres.

I stood
on this cold battlefield
choking on fear
and the February air

walked
between the silent blocks
the steel-grilled shops
the streets shuttling
endlessly
back into each other —
I felt that we were
strapped tight
hurtling towards
some moment in space and time
we could not construe
or else that this speed
was the illusion of stasis
there was no escape
no meaning
in this prison
of concrete and night
— I lit cigarettes
and smoked them
to communicate
with some
heroic spirit
remembered from my childhood
— I consoled myself
with the sound
of my steel-heeled boots
on the plates
of the railway bridge

SEA FISHING

We knelt on the back-door steps
Banging sparks out of cement
With heavy hammers and strips of lead
Which we bent and folded in clumsy lumps
And boiled in a blackened pan
Huddled round like alchemist's apprentices
To watch its shabby dull grey surface
Wrinkle and soften and shine forth
Suddenly into miraculous molten silver
Which hissed and globbed in the holes
We molded in tins of wet sand
To harden and dull once more, but now
Transformed, shaped to our purpose;
The day when we'd make our way
To the water's edge, to lean against
The wind and cast our weights out far
Into the inscrutable sea, to wait
For the answering tug,
Men with a raison d'etre;
To coax from the ocean's leaden bass
A single, gleaming, note
A silver-scaled bass.

THE EAST WIND

Straight from Siberia, our mothers said,
The East wind blew in off the Irish Sea
To freeze us between the rows of houses
Where we ran in the glaring yellow light
To chase a dirty white plastic ball
Skittering along the concrete.

Our faces were frozen in monkey grins,
Our hands were completely numb
And when we fell flying onto the pavement
We did not feel a thing, nor stop
To check our limbs, but struggled up
To woodenly run on, not thinking
Of the relief and pain that would come
With the thaw.

INTENSITY, EXALTATION
after Vallejo

I want to write, but I foam at the mouth
There's so much to say but I get bogged down;
There's no number uttered which isn't a sum,
No pyramid written without a green heart.

I want to write, but I sense the puma;
I ask for laurel, but they give me an onion.
There's no sound made which doesn't grow vague,
There's neither god nor son of god without development.

So come on then, let's eat grass,
Fruit of weeping, flesh of moans,
Jam made out of our melancholy souls.

Come on! Come on! I am wounded;
Let's drink what's already been turned into piss,
Come on, mister crow, let's go to your missus.

NATURE POEM

Raindrops
Carved
The surface of the lake
Into the spiralled lid
Of a newgrange tomb
And I was filled with boredom
And great unsayables

The trees thrashed
In the wind
And crazily running
A butterfly (white)
Flew against my chest
And stuttered off

Stunned, I stood still
Hearing
Rain become aria

ELEGY FOR THE UNKNOWN SOLDIER

"It is hard to read on the ancient stone . . .
In the month of Athyr Levkios fell asleep."
— Cavafy

One evening in August, the light already failing
An insurance salesman dropped me off at a crossroads
In Cavan or Monaghan, the beginning of the drumlin country
I stood there for a while, near a newly-built bungalow
Watching the green fields darken behind a screen of hedges.
Just where the roads met there was a sort of green
With a JCB parked right up on the verge
And a small celtic cross of grey granite.
I walked over to read the inscription
Peering through the fading light.
"Patrick O'Neill, Volunteer, Third Belfast Brigade
Shot on a nearby hillside. 16 April 1923."
I can't remember exactly, but that was the gist of it.
By the time I finished reading, it was completely dark.
All the lights were on in the nearby bungalow,
I could see the TV screen through the living-room window.
I heard the engine of a car in the distance,
The cone of its headlights appearing and disappearing.
He stopped and gave me a lift to Cootehill. I didn't look back.

Lotharingen! Lotharingen!
Wagnerian anvil ringing
The steel hammer swinging
Into silence; which advances
Softly in suede shoes
Till the men hear nothing
But the sudden unheard beating
Of their own hearts. Maybe, then,
They begin to think
Of those who went before them
Who barely emerged from the clay
Before returning to blacken it
With their charred bodies
Leaving no memorial behind
But the steel and coal dust
Seeping out of flesh and bones
To rot their coffins overnight
And above them, stretched out
Like Finn across the landscape
A corpse that won't rot away
But pounded and tempered and soaked
Contorts into shapes of unplanned
Beauty, a dead black flower
From which they fall,
Slowly yellowing.

MADRUGADA

For years I lay awake in the darkness
Savouring a secret life after midnight
Ear pressed to the heart of Europe
Softly thundering distant music,
Slurred insomniac lullabies
For complex children.

Turning it off to sleep
I saw the dial's red glow
In after-image all around me
Like the votive lamp that burned
In my grandmother's kitchen.

Or sometimes I fell asleep
And woke with the radio still on
Batteries running down
Hissing absence into the light
Like a worn-out tradition.

Waking in darkness!
As if in the grip of forgotten habit
Like a character in a novel's
Opening paragraph, I am blind
Standing in my own light.

THE BLACK PIANO

The language turns to mush in our mouths —
Like the brown slush flooding the streets
Beneath my window. But now it's snowing,
White flakes falling on the frozen canals.
In my room, I turn the pages of Russian books
Trying to understand, knowing
That the storm that swept them away
Is the storm that swept me here
To stand in the place where they once stood
My head ringing with their echoes.
Through the wall of my room I hear
The tuneless tentative notes
Of my neighbour's pupils,
Their fingers stumbling over the keyboard.
Coming home late at night, I like
To climb the steps and peer
Into her tiny front room,
Filled with a frozen black piano
Basted with hidden light, like a shrine.
In my room I stalk on,
Imagining listeners behind the white wall
Their ears bent to the tuneless tentative sound
Of my black boots plodding through virgin snow.

VALPARAISO

He sat in the gloom like a dim buddha
His bald oval head gleaming
In the faint light filtering into the room.
There was a smell of damp earth in the hallway
The heavy long sadness of ancient forest floors
Where the sun has never shone. We entered
From the chilly marble stairs, still splashed
With light and shouts from the street outside
And stumbled over the screens and tapestries
Low sofas festooned with Indian designs
That he patiently crafted here, in the back streets
Of a tourist town.
                      He was no Indian, though silent
And patient as one, and his large brown eyes
Were like the stolen eggs of some exotic bird
That dreams of mountains and circling, circling
Through brilliant skies. The light
Assaulted the blinds that hadn't been open in years
Filtering into the room in slits
Illuming snatches of dust.
Someone whispered his story in my ear, the usual
One I'd heard before; economist
In the Allende government, flight and exile,
His wife had left him for a minor diplomat,
Leaving him with children behind.
But none of this seemed relevant to his immobile
Vegetable sadness, which raddled the air
Like a dry stain. His son put on his leather jacket
Went out to hunt *rubias* in the local discos
Up on the roof I bounced a ball
With his neurotic daughter
Her vowels already rounded by Catalan.
Later that night, Luis arrived to cook the meat.
Nervy, garrulous, Argentinian,
Cursing Spain and leaving it behind him,

His tickets home already bought.
We talked about Borges and Spanish football
Our faces red with the heat of the coals
While down in the streets, the tourists drifted
Through valleys of floodlit sculptured flowers.
I woke next morning before anyone else,
And padded through the hallway. Through the open door
I saw him laid on his bed like a toppled idol,
Barely breathing, in the other bed his daughter
Restless and creased, a dark snake in the undergrowth.
The light drilled into the walls. Outside,
It was Sunday on the beach, the trains
Came lurching and rocking out of Barcelona
Searing in the heat, packed with people
Their limbs already turning brown.
Before we left that afternoon
We sat once more in the gloom to sing some songs
And he strummed a simple melancholy dance
Over and over again, on the strung shell of a armadillo,
And falling through the years,
I saw a winter's morning of fear and booming voices
My hands cold clutching the varnished wood
While I painfully glossed a Gaelic poem
About a ship sailing out of Valparaiso
And how its purple echo had sailed with me
To this strange harbour, this unmapped land,
To dance now to the Charrango!

ANNE FRANK

(What we cannot speak about,
we must pass over in silence . . .)

Life is lived in rooms like this.
That, at least, we can say.
And people come and go
On speakable missions,
Clear commands. And we can talk
And smother the air with words
Till we feel we understand.

In these rooms we sleep and dream,
And rise to breakfast on white linen.
There are books to read,
And at night the scratch
Of pen and paper.

Life is lived in rooms like this
Where we lean towards a square of light
But where the walls are
We can only discover
By walking out into that darkness
Fingers outstretched, blind
Knowing we have no words
For what we may find.

EXILES

In all the dead ends of Dublin
you will find the Italian chippers
abandoned, forgotten consulates
of obscure Apenine villages
whose chocolate-box picture
sometimes hangs
above the bubbling friers.
Again and again,
they dispense our visas
sealed with salt and vinegar
wrapped in greaseproof paper.
Somehow we never go.

The old consul
has grown sardonic.
He stares out the steamed-up
windows at the rain,
the file of bored taximen
waiting at the rank.
His eyes glint with vendetta.
He lights up another Sweet Afton

turns to glare at his sons
who have mastered the local dialect,
leaning across the counter
to chat with their friends.
Sometimes, without warning
they all begin
to shout in Italian
like Joyce and his children.

ON HEARING MICHAEL HARTNETT
READ HIS POETRY IN IRISH

First, the irretrievable arrow of the military road
Drawing a line across all that has gone before
It's language a handful of brutal monosyllables.

By the side of the road the buildings eased up;
The sturdy syntax of castle and barracks
The rococo flourish of a stately home

The formal perfection and grace
Of the temples of neoclassical government
The avenues describing an elegant period. Then,

The red-brick constructions of a common coin
To be minted in local stone, and beyond them
The fluent sprawl of the demotic suburbs

Tanged with the ice of its bitter nights
Where I dreamt in the shambles of imperial iambs,
Like rows of shattered Georgian houses.

I hear our history on my tongue,
The music of what has happened!
The shanties that huddled around the manor

The kips that cursed under Christchurch Cathedral
Rising like a madrigal into the Dublin sky
— But tonight, for the first time,

I heard the sound
Of the snow falling through moonlight
Onto the empty fields.

LATIN AS A FOREIGN LANGUAGE

I suppose I should feel somehow vindicated
        To see our declensions bite deeper
            Than our legionaries' swords —
                But somehow I don't.
            We're a mixed lot here, devils
        To drink; old senatorial types and
Discarded favourites, poets without patrons etc.

When asked why they're here they might answer
        About duty to the empire, missionary zeal
            Or simply the spirit of adventure —
                All rot, of course.
            No one leaves Rome unless
        He has to, or not exactly because he has to
Like a vulgar soldier in a conscripted legion.

But things somehow *conspire* to force him out.
        Not all poets find patrons, not all
            Fit smoothly into public life —
                You know how it is.
            One wrong word in the wrong ear.
        One fateful opportunity fluffed, and
You may as well forget it. Who understands these things?

Some say they lie in the lap of the gods but either way
        We end up here in the backwaters of the empire
            Drumming our illustrious tongue
                Into barbarian skulls
            And polishing up the phrases
        Of the oafs who govern in Rome's name.
Like I said, a mixed lot, refugees all from obscure failures.

Some marry local girls, and sprout blonde beards
        And curls overnight. Poor bastards!
            How can they take seriously

Those bovine bodies
Those gaudy faces lisping bad breath.
Who could write poetry for such as these?
I think about these things a lot, but come to no conclusion.

During the freezing winter nights sitting round the wine
And olives, telling tales of sunnier days
Sucking ancient bits of gossip
Down to the dry pit
Cato elaborates his pet theory;
How Rome will someday crumble to dust
Beneath the barbarian heel, and only our precious language

Will survive, a frail silken line flung across the years.
But I don't know. Who among these barbarians
Would give a fart in his bearskin
For Horace or Virgil
Or any of us? All they want is enough
To haggle with a Sicilian merchant, or cheat
The Roman tax collector out of his rightful due.

But late at night, when I stumble out into
The sleet and cold I was not born to
And feel the threatening hug
Of those massive forests
Stuffed with nameless beasts
And the great godless northern sky
Threatening me with its emptiness and indifference

To me and all that are like me — then, sometimes,
I think he may be right; that
We are the galley slaves
Sweating below
Bearing the beautiful
Princess who sits in the prow
Across the ocean to her unknown lover.

THE REAL THING

I shuffled the musty floorboards
Of your emporium, stuffed with baubles
And useless knick-knacks, melancholy
Mechanical toys from Hong Kong, that soon
Fell asunder, scattering pieces of coloured tin
And stone-age plastic all over the house,
Like indecipherable relics.

Where did you come from? I like
To think of you, a grey-bearded shuffler
Peddling your goods all round the Baltic
From Lübeck and Lublin to Dublin
Where the pale children from the nameless suburbs
Gawked at your gaudy mortal balloons
Their fingers and eyes hungry for gewgaws.

After the war, you imported thousands
Of plywood fiddles, and sold them
At half-a-crown apiece, to some old fiddler;
Who would take them and bury them in shallow
Graves, in the uncertain soil of Dublin gardens
For six months or more, to resurrect them
Like Viking bones, grown moldy and seasoned
Their ears clogged with gritty earth;
To sell them all summer long
At feises and fleadhs all over the country.
And no one could tell them from the real thing.

GLASNEVIN CEMETERY

With deportment learnt from samurai films
I surface in the ancestral suburbs.
My grandmother is older than China,
Wiser than Confucius.
I pace my stride to hers
Soaking in the grey-green air.

Under my name cut in stone
My grandfather lies
Within hearing of the lorries roar
Out on the main road.
I forget my unseemly haste
To see the Emperor's tomb.

We search for family graves
In the suburbs of the dead.
From the jumble of worn stones
Unmarked by celtic crosses
Like an egyptologist she elucidates
Obscure back-street dynasties.

We see where Parnell lies buried
Under Sisyphean stone
Put there my father says
To keep him from climbing out.
I am surprised by ancient bitterness
Surfacing among the TV programmes.

The plotters of the nation
Are niched in their kitsch necropolis.
Matt Talbot, Larkin, Michael Collins
A holy graven trio
Shoulder to shoulder enshrined
In the tidy bogomil parlour of her heart.

The day flowers sluggishly
From the stone of contradictions.
The trees sway like green hasidim
I shuffle in a kind of lethargic dance
A sprung sign among the signified
A tenant in the suburbs of silence.